Written By Susan K. Tolley
as told by Adolph Brown

Illustrated by Chad Cox

ISBN: 1475159102
ISBN-13: 9781475159103

My name is Adolph Brown. I'm grown up now, but I wasn't always.

I went to Newtown Rd. Elementary. I know I'm supposed to say I liked reading and math the best, but I didn't. I loved p.e.

The p.e. teacher helped me learn to run faster, she taught me to walk all the way across the gym walking on my hands. She taught me to do pull ups. Boy could I do pull ups.

I loved p.e. and lunch...especially pizza days.

I always got an "S" in behavior. I guess I wasn't an angel, cause I never got an "O." Then again, I never got an "N" or a "U" either. My mom would have been really mad at me if I brought home an "N" and really, really mad at me if I brought home a "U!"

I didn't want to disappoint my mom. She worked hard. She always worked two jobs, sometimes three jobs.

See, we were poor. No one knew where our dad went. He just left one day. There were five of us kids. We lived in a small apartment, and my mom worked all those jobs so she could pay for the apartment, and food, and clothes for us.

I know now we were poor. But I didn't much know it when I was a kid. My mother was always cheerful. She woke me up every morning saying, "It's gonna be a GREAT day!"

One day, it wasn't a great day. Two men came to our door and told my momma that my older brother, Oscar, had been killed.

That was the saddest day EVER for all of us. My grandfather and my Aunt Lorraine helped us. My teachers helped us, but it was a long time before my mother said, "It's gonna be a great day" again. It was a long time before we felt it was a great day.

I went on to junior high. Sometimes I got in trouble. I didn't always pick the best friends. I did a lot of "hanging out." I didn't always do my homework or my schoolwork.

One day my mother sat me down and told me how disappointed she was with me. She told me I had a good mind, and I was wasting it. Then she said something that really startled me.

She was crying and she said, "Adolph, I don't think I could stand it if two more men come to my house to tell me YOU are dead. And if you don't stop hanging out with the wrong kids and if you don't put your schoolwork first, that's what's gonna happen!"

Then my momma put her head on the table and sobbed and sobbed.

I didn't know quite what to do. She was crying so hard she didn't even hear me get up. I went to my room and thought and thought. I liked that my momma thought I had a good mind. Teachers had told me that too. Maybe I really did.

Two things happened the very next day. My mom woke me up for the first time in a very long time by saying, "It's gonna be a Great day!" And I paid attention in school and finished all my work and even did my homework.

I kept thinking I had a good mind, and I kept working hard at school. My grades started going up.

Some of my "friends" dropped me, mostly cause I didn't hang out after school. I joined the track team and worked on running faster, and I tried the pole vault.

When I got to high school, I really stayed focused. I put my name on the ballot to become class president, and I WON! I stayed on the track team and even set a record for the pole vault.

Girls liked me; I learned to dance. I found out I could dance really good!

When it came time to go to college, I chose the College of William and Mary. They even gave me a scholarship so I wouldn't have to pay for college or for where I lived while I was there. The scholarship was because my grades were so good.

I stayed in school until I earned the highest degree they offer…a doctorate. I was so excited when I got that diploma. My mother was proud, my sisters were proud, and by then I was married and my wife was proud. Most of all, I was proud!

Now I go traveling to lots of schools and remind students to be proud, to work hard and to read lots of books. I know if I could do it, all kids can do it. I almost always show students two things.

I show students the cap and gown that I wore when I graduated and became Dr. Adolph Brown.

And I show them I can still dance!

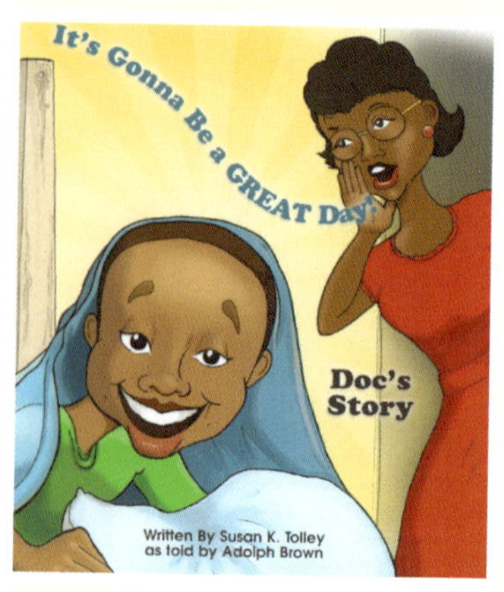

About the Book

It's Gonna Be a Great Day: Doc's Story is an uplifting story of fortitude and personal achievement written for children. Against many obstacles and gritty circumstances, young Adolph Brown succeeds and becomes a role model and inspiration for others. The book is inspiring and heartening.

About Adolph Brown

Adolph is a consultant and trainer in the areas of student achievement, school improvement, and service. His mission in life is to help others succeed. One of his favorite years in education was the year he was in Mrs. Tolley's third grade class. Doc is happily married with children ranging in age from 9 years old to 22 years old.

About Susan Tolley

Susan is an educator with over 33 years of experience in education. She has been a teacher, central office administrator, assistant principal, and principal. One of her favorite years in education was the year Adolph was in her third grade class. Now retired, Susan cherishes her job as "Aunt Susan" to Gabie and Michael and "Ganny" to Zack and Will.

About Chad Cox

Chad Cox is owner of 3 Waves Media, a design studio in Virginia. When he's not designing company websites for his clients, you will find him drawing or painting.